Drawing Together to Learn about
Feelings

Written by Marge Eaton Heegaard

To be illustrated by children
to help families communicate and learn together

Published by Fairview Press, 2450 Riverside Avenue, Minneapolis, Minnesota 55454.

Fairview Press is a division of Fairview Health Services, a community-focused health system affiliated with the University of Minnesota providing a complete range of services, from the prevention of illness and injury to care for the most complex medical conditions.

For a free current catalog of Fairview Press titles, please call toll-free 1-800-544-8207. Or visit our Web site at www.fairviewpress.org.

First printing: November 2003
ISBN-10: 1-57749-136-X
ISBN-13: 978-1-57749-136-1

Cover by Laurie Ingram Design (www.laurieingramdesign.com)
Interior by Dorie McClelland, Spring Book Design (www.springbookdesign.com)

We gratefully acknowledge the following individuals for their expertise and encouragement: Barbara Eckholdt, Carole Gesme, Judith Rubin, and Christy Pettitt. We thank Maria, Katie, Alex, David, Sara, Courtney, Amber, Bridget, and the children in the Friendship Group for testing this book and helping to make it better.

About this book

This book will help children and adults work together to understand and share feelings. It teaches healthy concepts while encouraging appropriate self-expression and concern for the feelings of others. It is designed for children ages six through twelve to illustrate with pictures they choose to draw. Younger children may need help understanding some of the words and concepts in the book, but do not offer too many suggestions. This is their book; let them make their own decisions about what to draw or write.

I recommend that a child be given a small box of new crayons to illustrate the book. While many children enjoy drawing with markers, crayons often encourage greater self-expression. Older children may prefer colored pencils.

Younger children like to illustrate books because images come more naturally to them than words. Older children are more comfortable expressing themselves verbally and may use words with their illustrations.

As you work through this book, focus on ideas and expression rather than drawing ability. Do not try to protect the child from difficult feelings. As children learn to understand and express their feelings, they develop life-long coping skills. If a drawing reveals that the child has misperceived something, correct the child gently. Remember that what a child perceives to be real is as powerful to that child as any reality.

Periodically invite the child to tell you more about his or her drawings. At the end of each section, you might explain something you have learned and ask the child to tell you something he or she has learned. When the book is completed, encourage the child to share his or her work with another adult for review and continued learning. Save the book as a keepsake of childhood memories.

Adults can help children understand feelings

Until recently, society encouraged people to repress unpleasant feelings, and many adults still have trouble sharing their emotions. Today, children are learning to recognize and verbalize feelings in school. They need parents and other adults to help them understand emotions and model acceptable forms of expression. They also need to develop sensitivity to the feelings of others.

Parents may be unaware of a child's emotions. Children often go into their rooms to cry alone, or act out feelings in problematic behaviors that seem unconnected with any recent event. It is important for children to express their feelings, especially at times of divorce, illness, death, and other changes. If they are unable to express grief, they may learn unhealthy ways of coping.

Magical thinking and a false sense of power over events may leave young children feeling guilty about things they did or did not do. They can learn to share feelings of guilt and accept that bad thoughts do not make bad things happen.

Shy children find it difficult to develop social skills and often feel unhappy about being alone. Parents must acknowledge these feelings and provide opportunities for socialization while children are young.

Anger is another difficult emotion. Young children first feel anger in the mouth, hands, or feet. They may want to bite, yell, hit, or kick. When they learn this isn't acceptable, they begin to repress their feelings, stuffing them in the stomach, head, or back. This leads to aches and pains.

Painful feelings will not just go away. Avoidance complicates feelings, but sharing draws people together. The Feelings Person exercise in this book will teach children and adults to more easily recognize their emotions. Once feelings are experienced internally, they can be released in appropriate ways.

This book is intended to help children:

To children

This is your book. You will make it different from all other books by drawing your own thoughts and feelings. You do not need any special skills to illustrate the pages. Just use lines, shapes, and colors to draw the pictures that come into your head as you read the words on each page.

Begin with the first page and do the pages in order. Ask an adult for help with words or pages you do not understand. When you have done a few pages, stop and share your work with an adult who cares about you.

Everyone has all kinds of feelings and they are all O.K. It is what you do with them that matters. You can control your behavior.

I hope you will have fun with this book while learning to accept and express your feelings and care about the feelings of others.

Feelings come from what I see and think. They may show on my face.

(Draw some feeling faces.)

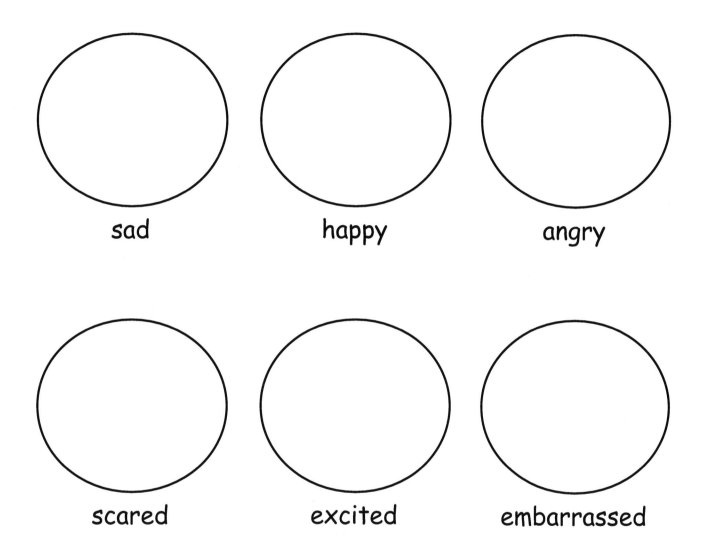

sad   happy   angry

scared   excited   embarrassed

Feelings are all O.K. Feelings are important.

Feelings affect the way I act. People who have the same feelings may act differently.

(Check ✓ what you do.)

When Shy

_____ I keep away

_____ I stay and act silly

_____ I act unfriendly

_____ I try to meet others

When Nervous

_____ I talk too much

_____ I stay very quiet

_____ I talk about it to someone

When Sad

_____ I just get quiet

_____ I cry

_____ I hit or break things

When Confused

_____ I pretend to know

_____ I ask questions

_____ I act as if I don't care

When Angry

_____ I cry

_____ I run away or hide

_____ I stay and fight

_____ I yell and holler

_____ I keep anger inside

When Frightened

_____ I run away

_____ I hide

_____ I get angry

Sometimes I hide difficult feelings by pretending to feel something else—almost like wearing a mask.

(Draw and name three feelings you try to hide.)

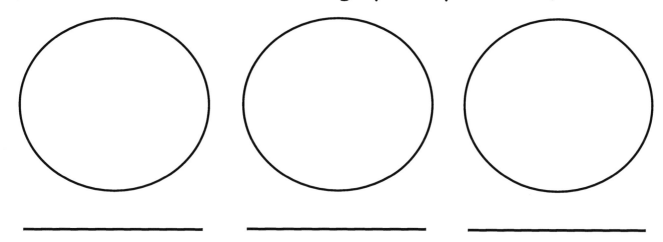

_____   _____   _____

(Draw and name the mask you use to hide each feeling.)

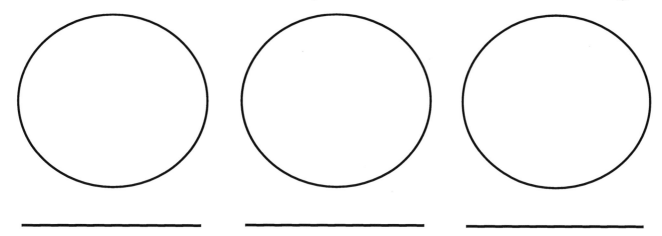

_____   _____   _____

Masks can build walls between you and others. They make it harder for others to get to know you.

When I don't want anyone to see me cry, I go somewhere else.

(Draw a picture of where you go to hide your crying.)

No one can comfort you if you cry alone. Crying to let sadness and pain out is always O.K.

I remember a time I felt very happy.
(Draw that time.)

It is good to remember happy times and happy feelings.

Feelings are something I feel in my body.

(Close your eyes and think of a feeling. Where in your body do you feel this feeling? Use the colors below.)

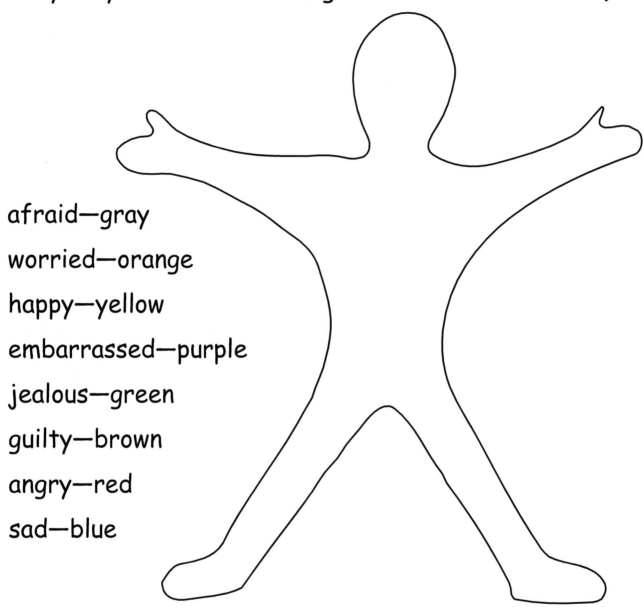

afraid—gray

worried—orange

happy—yellow

embarrassed—purple

jealous—green

guilty—brown

angry—red

sad—blue

It is important to know what you are feeling. Feelings affect your behavior.

If feelings are kept stuffed inside, they can cause aches and pains.

(Use red to color the places you get aches and pains.)

Look on page 6 to see which feelings you stuff in these places.

Everyone has feelings. You don't have to hide them.

There are two kinds of feelings. Pleasant (+) feelings feel good and give you energy. Unpleasant (–) feelings do not feel good and use up energy.

(Put a + or – after each of the following sentences.)

How would you feel if you:

Forgot your homework?

Made a big mistake?

Finished all your chores?

Had a fight with your brother or sister?

Did well on a spelling test?

Got a present from your grandparents?

Broke someone else's toy?

Had spinach for dinner?

Told a lie and did not get caught?

Got an invitation to a party?

Felt mad at a good friend?

Were teased by some big kids?

Happy and unhappy times are part of life.

Unpleasant feelings also serve a purpose.

FEAR is unpleasant, but it can warn you against danger.

GUILT is unpleasant, but it tells you when you did something wrong and need to change.

ANGER is unpleasant, but it can give you strength to protect yourself and others.

SADNESS is painful and unpleasant, but grieving brings healing.

It is possible to feel pleasant and unpleasant feelings at the same time. For example, you might feel both sad and happy about moving. You might feel excited about a new place, but a little afraid, too. You might be proud that you got an "A," but feel guilty because you cheated on the test.

People do many things to try to avoid unpleasant feelings.

They pretend something is different.

They think different thoughts.

They blame others.

They avoid things that seem uncomfortable.

They buy things.

They keep too busy.

They eat more and more often.

They use drugs or alcohol.

What do you do? _____

_____

These can become habits that are very hard to change. They are called DEFENSES because they are like shields that block unpleasant feelings. But they can also block pleasant feelings. It is important to feel all feelings.

I felt proud when I did something well that was hard to do.

(Draw a picture of something you are proud of.)

It is important to feel good about yourself and the things you do well.

There are people I love and like to be with.

(Draw a picture of some people you love.)

Love is a pleasant feeling. You can share your feelings with people you love.

I am excited about something I did or will soon do.

(Draw a picture.)

It is fun to share good feelings.

I have courage and feel brave when I try something new.

(Draw a picture of a time you tried something new.)

Everyone needs to try new foods and new skills. Nothing happens without trying.

I feel special when it is my birthday.

(Draw something else that helps you feel special.)

You are unique. There is no one else just like you.

Sometimes I feel disappointed.

(Draw a time you felt disappointed because something you wanted did not happen.)

There are times when all you can do is share your feelings and make the best of what happened.

There was a time I felt very angry at someone in my family.

(Draw a picture about that time.)

Most people feel angry sometimes at the people they love. It is O.K. to have angry feelings.

There are times that I feel bad about something I did or did not do. Feelings of guilt can be worse than punishment.

(Draw something you feel guilty about.)

You can learn from your mistakes. No one is perfect. It helps to apologize and talk about what you can do to make things better.

Sometimes I get really scared or have scary dreams.

(Draw a dream or a time you felt scared. Then, add a picture of someone or something to help you feel safe.)

Fear is a natural feeling. Drawing a fear may make it seem smaller and less powerful.

Grief is the word for the many feelings people get when they lose someone or something important.

(Draw a loss that you have many feelings about.)

What did you feel? _____

What did you do? _____

Did someone try to comfort you? _____

It helps to share these feelings with someone.

I remember feeling really embarrassed about something I did.

(Draw a picture about it.)

Sometimes we have to laugh at ourselves. It is O.K.

I worry quite often about something.
(Draw a picture about it.)

It helps to talk to someone about the things you worry about.

When others are gone or busy, I feel lonely.
(Draw a picture about a time you felt lonely.)

Reading a good book or playing with a favorite toy or stuffed animal can help you feel less alone.

I often feel shy in new places or around people I don't know.

(Draw a time you felt shy.)

Everyone feels shy sometimes. They are often afraid of saying or doing something wrong. You can learn to be brave and try something new or meet new people.

Sometimes when I try to do something that is really difficult, I feel frustrated.

(Draw a time you felt frustrated.)

Remember, you can always ask someone for help. The worse failure might be to never try.

When someone can have or do something that I cannot, I feel jealous.

(Draw someone or something that makes you feel jealous.)

There is a difference between needs and wants. It is important to have your needs met, but no one can have all their wants met.

When my feelings are too many or too painful, I have a place where I can go to feel comfortable and safe.

(Draw a place where you feel good.)

Feelings often change when you stop thinking about them and do something else for a while.

There are times I feel very helpless and don't know what to do.

(Draw a time you felt this way.)

You can ask for help. Learning more about something helps you feel more powerful.

I have done things that seem to make others feel uncomfortable.

(Draw something you did and how the other person felt.)

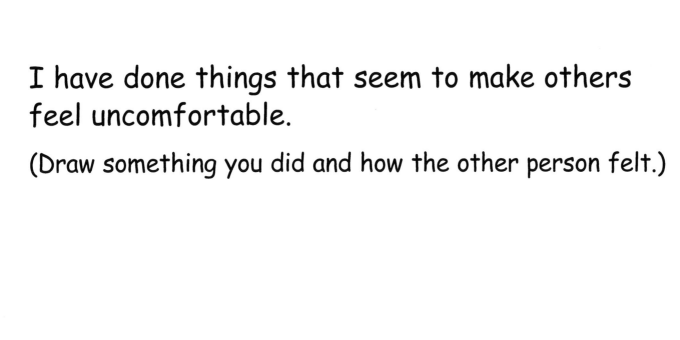

It is very important to think about the feelings of others.

Children cannot always say or do what they are thinking or feeling.

Babies cry to get their needs met because they have not learned to talk. Older children can use words to ask for what they need, but crying is O.K. to let sadness out.

Toddlers may yell, kick, or hit when they feel angry. When they get older, they learn to use words and say "I am angry because . . ." so they don't get punished for bad behavior.

Children can learn how to manage feelings so they can feel better without hurting others.

There are many good ways to let feelings out.
(Check ✓ what you do.)

_____ Paint with watercolors to let sadness out.

_____ Write in a journal.

_____ Draw pictures.

_____ Exercise or play sports.

_____ Walk or run.

_____ Shout into a pillow.

_____ Play a musical instrument.

_____ Clean my room.

_____ Say "I am feeling . . ."

_____ Play with my toys.

_____ Tear up old newspapers.

_____ Do something nice for someone.

Feelings just happen, but you can choose your behavior.

I am learning to understand feelings and can share them with others. I feel good about that.

(Draw a picture of yourself.)

The best feeling is often feeling good about yourself.

Name_____

Address_____

_____

Phone Number_____ Age_____